Math Around Us

Using Subtraction at the Park

Tracey Steffora

Heinemann Library
Chicago, Illinois

www.capstonepub.com
Visit our website to find out more information about Heinemann-Raintree books.

To order:
☎ Phone 800-747-4992
▭ Visit www.capstonepub.com to browse our catalog and order online.

© 2011 Heinemann Library
an imprint of Capstone Global Library, LLC
Chicago, Illinois

Edited by Rebecca Rissman, Tracey Steffora, and Catherine Veitch
Designed by Joanna Hinton-Malivoire
Picture research by Elizabeth Alexander
Production by Victoria Fitzgerald
Originated by Capstone Global Library Ltd
Printed in the United States of America in
Eau Claire, Wisconsin. 021916 009517RP

15 14 13
10 9 8 7 6 5 4

Library of Congress Cataloging-in-Publication Data
Steffora, Tracey.
  Using subtraction at the park / Tracey Steffora.
    p. cm.—(Math around us)
  Includes bibliographical references and index.
  ISBN 978-1-4329-4925-9 (hc)—ISBN 978-1-4329-4933-4
(pb) 1. Subtraction—Juvenile literature. I. Title.
  QA115.S7776 2011
  513.2′12—dc22   2010030769

Acknowledgments
The author and publisher are grateful to the following for permission to reproduce photographs: © Capstone Publishers pp. 18, 19, 20 (Karon Dubke); Alamy pp. 4 (© PCL), 5 (© Gregory Wrona), 6 (© Andy Salter), 10 (© Tracey Foster), 22 (Paul Springett 02); Corbis p. 14 (© moodboard); Shutterstock pp. 7 (© Paula Cobleigh), 9 (© Manamana), 11 (© Mircea Bezergheanu), 13 (© Kheng Guan Toh), 15 (© c.), 15 (© marre), 15 background (© val lawless), 16 (© c.), 16 (© marre), 16 background (© val lawless), 21 (© David P. Lewis), 23 glossary – marble (© marre), 23 glossary – squirrel (© Paula Cobleigh), 23 glossary – swan (© Kheng Guan Toh).

Cover photograph of children playing hide-and-seek in the park reproduced with permission of Photolibrary (Juice Images). Back cover photograph of a gray squirrel reproduced with permission of Shutterstock (© Paula Cobleigh).

We would like to thank Nancy Harris, Dee Reid, and Diana Bentley for their assistance in the preparation of this book.

Every effort has been made to contact copyright holders of material reproduced in this book. Any omissions will be rectified in subsequent printings if notice is given to the publisher.

Contents

At the Park

A park is a busy place.

People come and go at the park.

Animals come and go at the park.

Take One Away

There are two squirrels in the grass.

One squirrel runs up a tree.
How many are left?

Start with two. Take one away.

There is one squirrel left.

Take Two Away

There are four swans in the water.

Two swans fly away.

How many are left?

Start with four. Take two away.

There are two swans left.

Take Three Away

Some children are playing marbles.

How many marbles are in this circle?

What if three are hit out of the circle?

Start with six. Take three away.

Six take away three equals three.

$$6 - 3 = 3$$

There are three marbles left.

Three children are on the swings.

All three children leave.

How many children are left?

$$3 - 3 = 0$$

There are no children left on the swings.

It is time to go home. Tomorrow will
be another day at the park!

Subtraction Story

Look at the picture. Can you write your own subtraction story?

Picture Glossary

marble a small glass ball used to play games

squirrel an animal that has a bushy tail and strong back legs

swan a large water bird with a long neck

Index

Notes to Parents and Teachers

Before reading

Familiarize children with the language of subtraction by inviting four children to stand up. Then ask one child to walk away. Say "We started with four. One went away. How many are left?" Repeat with different numbers of children or give children objects to manipulate as you familiarize them with the terms "take away" and "how many are left".

After reading

- Review the subtraction language presented in the book and the symbols associated with subtraction sentences or equations. Explain that another word for "take away" is "minus".

- Ask children to name other familiar playground games. Have them describe how to play the game and encourage them to think and identify if there are any instances of subtraction present while playing the games. With the children, write some subtraction stories and equations to go along with their descriptions.